Overview of Fujian Taizu Boxing

By
Zheng Jinbu (曾金卜)

Translated and annotated by Russ Smith

武林館

Overview
of
Fujian
Taizu Boxing

By
Zheng Jinbu (曾金卜)

Translated and annotated by Russ Smith

Burinkan Martial Arts
Martial Forest LLC

Disclaimer

The author and publisher of this book DISCLAIM ANY RESPONSIBILITY over any injury as a result of the techniques taught in this book. Readers are advised to consult a physician about their physical condition before undergoing any strenuous training or dangerous physical activity. This book details dangerous techniques that may cause serious physical injury and even death. Practice and training require a fit and healthy student and a qualified instructor.

Martial Forest LLC edition: 3/16/2023
©2022 Russ L. Smith

ISBN-13: 979-8-9873969-4-0
ISBN-10: 8-9873969-4-0

Photography by: Russ Smith
Edited by Russ Smith
Interior Design by: Russ Smith
Cover Design by: Russ Smith

Table of Contents

武

林

館

Acknowledgments

I would like to acknowledge and thank the following people for their support and encouragement over the years and during the creation of this book:

My wife, **Nicole**, who supported my trips overseas and across the country, and my fervent desire to train and study nights and weekends for decades. I would especially like to thank her for opening our home to visitors and making them feel welcome.

Sifu Mark Wiley, thank you for your friendship, and for sharing your vast knowledge of Five Ancestor boxing with me. Your examples of teaching from a principles-first approach have helped me grow in all the things that I do. I cannot thank you enough.

And lastly, but not least, I'd like to thank these fine martial artists for their assistance understanding, and translating Chinese terms into their useful and correct context:

- Sifu Dominic Lim
- Sensei Hing-Poon Chan
- Sifu David Wong
- Tory Ellarson
- Sifu Robert Chu
- Sifu Grant Brown

About the Book

Boxing manuals, known as quanpu (拳谱), are written records that document the techniques and principles of Southern Chinese martial arts. These manuals typically include illustrations and descriptions of various techniques and forms, as well as information about the history and philosophy of the martial art. Quanpu were used by martial artists as a reference for training and as a means of preserving and passing down the knowledge and techniques of the art. They were also used to share information between different schools and practitioners and to document the development of the art over time. Quanpu played a significant role in the development and preservation of Southern Chinese martial arts and continue to be an important resource for martial artists today.

We are planning on producing translations of additional quanpu in the future, including those related to Fujian White Crane, Five Ancestor Boxing, Shouting Crane, the boxing-related sections of the General Tian "Bubishi", the "Boxing Classic", and more.

The book you currently hold primarily consists of a translation of a small, unillustrated quanpu called "Overview of Taizu Boxing," which was written by Zheng Jinbu (曾金卜) for his student, Zheng Lianlai (郑连来). The book was later annotated and published by Zheng Lianlai, adding explanations for terms and phrases specific to Quanzhou martial arts. These explanations, along with the author's training in Fujian Five Ancestor Boxing (which contains Taizuquan) form the basis for the commentary that follows.

Even with numerous cross-references and experience training in related systems, translation efforts such as this rely upon personal interpretation and best-guess selection of options to be made by the translator. Others will likely have alternative approaches to the choices made by this translator. All mistakes are ours, and we welcome constructive feedback on this effort, and we hope other qualified translators will join in the effort of making this ancient wisdom more accessible to today's practitioners.

About Song Taizu, Zhao Kuangyin

Zhao Kuangyin (赵匡胤), eventually known as Song Taizu (宋太祖), was the founder of the Song dynasty in China and ruled as the first emperor from 960 to 976. He was born in the late 9th century in present-day Henan province as the younger brother of a military general.

Zhao joined the military at a young age and rose through the ranks due to his intelligence and bravery. He was eventually appointed as a commander and gained the support of his troops through his fair treatment of them. In 960, the ruling dynasty, the Zhou, was in a state of disarray and corruption, and Zhao saw an opportunity to seize power.

Zhao led a successful military campaign to capture the capital and declare himself emperor, thus establishing the Song dynasty. As emperor, Zhao implemented several reforms aimed at strengthening the government and improving the lives of the people. He introduced a new examination system for selecting government officials based on merit rather than birth or wealth, which helped to eliminate corruption and promote competent leaders. He also introduced a new law code to ensure fair treatment of the people and improve the administration of justice.

In addition to his political reforms, Zhao also supported the arts and culture of his time. He was a patron of literature and sponsored the creation of several works, including the famous "New History of the Tang Dynasty." He also encouraged the development of agriculture and commerce, which led to a period of prosperity and growth for the Song dynasty.

However, despite his many achievements, Zhao faced challenges during his reign, including several uprisings and invasions from neighboring kingdoms. He was able to effectively deal with these threats through his military prowess and diplomatic skills, but he died before he could fully resolve these issues.

Zhao's legacy has had a lasting impact on Chinese history. He is widely regarded as one of China's greatest emperors and is remembered for his military prowess, political reforms, and support of the arts. The Song dynasty that he founded lasted for over three centuries and was known for its economic and cultural achievements, making it one of the most important dynasties in Chinese history.

Zhao is believed to have had a significant influence on the development of Taizu boxing. It is believed that the style was developed by imperial guards who were loyal to Song Taizu and was used to protect the emperor and maintain order in the empire.

The influence of Taizu boxing can be seen in its migration to the Fujian province of China, where it became an important part of the local culture and was passed down from generation to generation. In Fujian, Taizu boxing was widely practiced by both civilians and military personnel, and it was considered an important aspect of their cultural heritage. The style was also used for self-defense and physical fitness, and it was often performed during festivals and other cultural events.

Today, Taizu boxing continues to be practiced in Fujian province, Taiwan, Singapore, and other parts of Southeast Asia, and it is considered an important part of China's cultural heritage.

The style remains popular among martial arts enthusiasts and continues to be taught and practiced by people from all walks of life.

About Taizuquan

太祖拳者, 少林一脉。
Taizu boxing, Shaolin lineage.

传自赵宋, 太祖匡胤。
Passed down from Zhao Song, Taizu Kuangyin.

Translator Commentary:

太祖拳者, 少林一脉。

Indicates the name and heritage of the art. In Chinese martial arts, it is common that all arts with any resemblance to Shaolin boxing are generally attributed to the Shaolin temple in some way.

传自赵宋, 太祖匡胤。

Gives specific homage to Zhao Kuangyin, given the posthumous title "Taizu" (Grand Ancestor), founder of the Song Dynasty (宋朝 years 960-1279).

单技独马, 天下无双。

One skill per stance, unparalleled in the world.

龙骧虎步, 帝王气象。

Dragon leaps and tiger steps, the atmosphere of the emperor.

Translator Commentary:

单技独马, 天下无双。

Taizu has a convention of execution that generally has one major arm movement per step or stance, relative to the rotation of the hips and the style's power development methodology.

This is indicated as a superior boxing method, demonstrating pride in the boxing tradition.

龙骧虎步, 帝王气象。

References to the dragon, tiger, and the image of the emperor are all made to invoke a feeling of respect and authority embodied in the tradition.

中权逼靠, 尺寸争锋。

Focused on the center, victory is seized over a short distance.

策近短打, 硬马硬截。

Approaching for a short strike, with a solid stance and crisp movements.

Translator Commentary:

中权逼靠, 尺寸争锋。

Southern Taizuquan focuses on attacking the opponent's centerline and approaching through the middle door (inside gate). Relative to Northern Taizuquan, Southern Taizuquan fights in a short distance.

策近短打, 硬马硬截。

To fight at short distances, a Taizu boxer must approach to an effective range, have a strong, rooted, stance, and be able to issue crisp power.

稳扎稳打，步步进前。
Stable in defense and steady in attack, moving straight forward.

技手分明，理法简约。
Skills are clear, principles and methods are concise.

Translator Commentary:

稳扎稳打，步步进前。

Stability and steadiness are indicators of the general nature of Taizuquan as a grounded boxing methodology.

Straight forward is the preferred direction of attack, advancing rather than retreating or evading.

技手分明，理法简约。

Taizuquan takes pride in being a straight-forward, clear, and powerful boxing method. With clarity of both purpose and training methods, it can be well understood, demonstrated, and taught.

刚柔相济，四术兼备。
Hard and soft cooperating, with the four skills combined.

吞吐浮沉，衍化无穷。
Swallow/Spit/Float/Sink, endlessly evolving.

Translator Commentary:

刚柔相济，四术兼备。

Hard and soft mutually assisting is a common phrase in Fujian martial traditions, indicating the importance of balancing hard and aggressive methods, with softer, yielding approaches.

"Four skills" is a reference to a wide variety of fighting methods.

Commonly called "ti, da, shuai, na", these are kicking, striking, takedowns, and grappling, respectively.

吞吐浮沉，衍化无穷。

Swallow, spit, float, and sink are important four-character concepts in nearly all Fujian martial traditions, referring to the four fundamental directions of energy (back, forward, up, and down).

势雄劲猛，力点分明。

Fierce and imposing momentum, expression of power is clear.

发拳响劲，穿壁洞石。

Punches are powerful enough to hear, and pierce through stone.

Translator Commentary:

势雄劲猛，力点分明。

Taizuquan is a relatively aggressive style with fast and powerful movements, typically delivered in a staccato fashion, rather than flowing and blending movements together. This makes it possible to see the practitioner's power clearly.

发拳响劲，穿壁洞石。

When a Taizuquan practitioner's power is developing, it becomes possible to hear the clothes whipping, and when sufficiently developed, one should hear a reverberation in the body, regardless of clothing.

"Piercing through stone" is a form of poetic hyperbole, meant to invoke a feeling of power.

门户严正, 矩镬肃谨。

Proper posture guards the door, with seriousness and restraint.

进退有规, 俯仰有矩。

There are rules for advancing and retreating, and guidelines for action.

Translator Commentary:

门户严正, 矩镬肃谨。

The proper body posture of Taizuquan is meant to contribute to the practitioner's defense, and should not be neglected.

进退有规, 俯仰有矩。

Taizuquan has strategies and tactics which serve to help the practitioner in both attacking and defending. These are meant to guide the boxer's actions.

前手如盾，后手如矛。
The front hand is like a shield, the rear hand is like a spear.

内蕴阴柔，外示阳刚。
Soft on the inside, hard on the outside.

Translator Commentary:

前手如盾，后手如矛。

In this Taizu manual, it is recommended to defend with the lead hand, and attack with the rear hand. It should be noted that some other manuals have this reversed.

内蕴阴柔，外示阳刚。

Taizu recommends that the external visage and form be hard, strong, and masculine, while the internal aspects are soft, fluid, and feminine.

一阴一阳, 变化无穷。

One yin and one yang, endless changes.

攻则硬猛, 守则密捷。

Attacking is hard and fierce, while defense is tight and quick.

Translator Commentary:

一阴一阳, 变化无穷。

Yin and yang, in this context, refers to many boxing concerns…long and short, high and low, defense and offense, straight and circular, hard and soft, and many more.

Successful boxers are able to transform quickly from one method to another to overwhelm an opponent and circumvent their defenses.

攻则硬猛, 守则密捷。

Fierceness denotes the bravery necessary to attack with speed and power, while an effective and fast defense is necessary for the practitioner's survival.

四正归中，墓牌身稳。
Recover to the center, with the stability of the tombstone body.

正气堂堂，易守中枝。
Upright and dignified, easy to defend the center.

Translator Commentary:

四正归中，墓牌身稳。

When extended in any direction, it becomes prudent to retract to the center, relying on a stable, straight torso to maintain the center of gravity.

Among Fujian boxing styles, this straight torso is likened to a tombstone…stable, straight, and difficult to move.

正气堂堂，易守中枝。

Taizu boxers believe that when one's posture is straight, as if dignified and proud, defending the center becomes easier.

三角势法, 便于进退。

Triangle body method, makes it easier to advance and retreat.

守势在前, 攻势在后。

The defense is in the front, the offense is behind.

Translator Commentary:

三角势法, 便于进退。

While the "tombstone body" is typically facing the opponent with the chest flat and belly-button pointed forward, the "triangle body" has the chest turned away from the opponent at approximately 45° angle.

This slightly-turned posture is often the end-result of expressing power with one of the hips, rotating it forward. With one hip forward and the other behind, quick stepping (either forward or back) is possible.

守势在前, 攻势在后。

Since the shoulders are typically aligned above the hips, the triangle body extends one shoulder and arm forward of the other, increasing its reach. This lead arm is typically given the role of defense, clearing a path for the rear hand to attack.

武林館

3

Advice on Posture

Posture of the head

> 头为身主, 气血会注。
>
> **The head is the master of the body, where the qi and blood are organized.**
>
> 诸经归之, 其容必正。
>
> **The meridians converge, and their content must be correct.**

Translator Commentary:

头为身主, 气血会注。

With the brain, eyes, and ears located in the head, the importance of the head cannot be over-stated. According to Traditional Chinese Medicine (TCM), the blood and qi are managed in the head.

诸经归之, 其容必正。

TCM describes that the qi meridians converge in the head, and the head is where the organization of function and equilibrium occur in the meridian channels.

头正身正，领起精神。
Head and body are upright, leading the spirit.

百会聚提，顶提头挺。
Baihui facing upward, the head is lifted.

Translator Commentary:

头正身正，领起精神。

Straightness is a primary characteristic of both the head and body. It is believed a person is only fully in control when the body and head are aligned vertically.

百会聚提，顶提头挺。

The Baihui point on the top of the head is expected to face upward and the head should have the feeling of being pulled upward.

> 咬齿龈根，筋起项强。
> **Gritting the teeth, put strength in the neck tendons.**
>
> 直项收颔，山根宜起。
> **Straighten the neck, retract the chin, and open the eyes wide.**

Translator Commentary:

咬齿龈根，筋起项强。

Because of the danger of being struck in the head and face, boxers are advised to close the mouth and tighten the muscles of the neck.

In some Fujian styles, this creates a strangely contorted face and mouth area, likened to a fish or the diety Kui Xing (魁星).

直项收颔，山根宜起。

Straightening and tightening the neck has the effect of protecting the throat, and pulling the chin backward. While doing this, the eyes should be opened wide to observe the opponent(s).

机锋在眼, 两目平视。
The eyes are sharp, gazing straight ahead.

眼观六路, 目光四射。
Looking at the six roads, the eyes radiate in all directions.

Translator Commentary:

机锋在眼, 两目平视。

Eyes should have a piercing stare, able to unnerve some opponents.

眼观六路, 目光四射。

With the eyes open wide, they will glimmer and be able to see even in the periphery.

眼神游移, 其心必怯。

If the eyes are wandering, the heart is timid.

目识无神, 其艺必浅

When the eyes lack spirit, the skills are likely shallow.

Translator Commentary:

眼神游移, 其心必怯。

The eyes can betray the mind. If one's eyes are looking all about in fear, looking for an avenue of escape, you can know they lack the confidence to succeed.

目识无神, 其艺必浅

This lack of confidence tells you that their skills are not sufficient to the task.

心定眼明, 瞥如飞鸿。

With a clear mind, and the vision of an eagle.

审度强弱, 俯仰高低。

Judging strengths and weaknesses, handling all things…high and low.

Translator Commentary:

心定眼明, 瞥如飞鸿。

A Taizu boxer should be calm and confident, looking objectively at every situation, not missing any details.

审度强弱, 俯仰高低。

This calm clarity provides the practitioner the ability to gauge each situation correctly, regardless of the problem. He will not miss any details of the upper or lower body, and will be able to ascertain the opponent's strengths and weaknesses and act appropriately.

目识神威, 敌情预晓。
Eyes are keen, predicting the enemy's situation.

耳听八方, 闻风而警。
Ears hear in all directions, senses maintaining alertness.

Translator Commentary:

目识神威, 敌情预晓。

Sharp eyes are critical to assessing an opponent.

耳听八方, 闻风而警。

Maintaining the ability to hear well under stress may be critical to survival in situations where the Taizu boxer is potentially outnumbered. Keeping attentive to all the senses may be critical to the boxer's survival.

Posture of the Torso

子午归中, 上下相对。

Return to the center line, keeping the top and bottom coordinated.

神完气足, 耳聪目明。

The spirit is full of energy, and the ears and eyes are sharp.

Translator Commentary:

子午归中, 上下相对。

Whenever extending, be sure to return to the center and to protect the center. The center of the body is where many of the opponent's targets reside, and any strikes he can make to the center are likely to penetrate deeply.

Keep the vertical equilibrium by keeping the Bai Hui point above the tailbone. This combination of a straight head and body provides the boxer coordinated freedom of movement.

神完气足, 耳聪目明。

When the body is well aligned, it is energetic, agile, and alert.

含胸拔背，卸肩插胛。

Contain the chest, round the back, sink the shoulders, and position the shoulder blades.

沉肘扣节，襟胸宜守

Sink the elbow joint and drop the wrist, the chest should be guarded.

Translator Commentary:

含胸拔背，卸肩插胛。

The shoulders should be dropped and rolled slightly forward, which rounds the back.

From that position, put strength in the latissimus dorsi muscles and this will rotate the scapula.

沉肘扣节，襟胸宜守

The elbow is sunk in front of the torso and the wrists dropped. The forearms protect the chest.

以肩带肘, 不逾子午。

Shoulder leads the elbow, which must manage the center line.

先软后硬, 前后叫应

Soft first and then hard, alternating and coordinating.

Translator Commentary:

以肩带肘, 不逾子午。

The action of the crotch turns the hip, the action of the hip turns the shoulder, and the action of the shoulder powers the elbow. The elbow manages the hand and the structure of the elbow to the tips of the fingers must protect the centerline.

先软后硬, 前后叫应

Issue power from a relaxed state, with both hands working in concert with one another as well as taking turns to manage the actions of the opponent.

节力沉实，策近靠打。

Conserve strength wisely, approaching close to fight.

体之所在，法宜活便。

When the body is trained, the methods are lively.

Translator Commentary:

节力沉实，策近靠打。

Boxers are advised to conserve their strength, so it can be fully available when closing the distance to attack. Do not bounce, show off, or otherwise waste time and motion which can give the opponent information about your capabilities. Find your opportunity, enter, and issue your power.

体之所在，法宜活便。

Follow the guidelines for posture and train hard. In doing so, you will develop the ability to be agile, effective, and adaptable.

> 外观四正, 内通八关。
>
> **Appear upright, and energy will flow unimpeded.**
>
> 身田端正, 坐节按力。
>
> **Body should be straight, with wrists sitting in preparation.**

Translator Commentary:

外观四正, 内通八关。

When the outer appearance has everything in order, then the body's energy will flow through all areas of the body.

身田端正, 坐节按力。

The body should be correct, with the wrists sunk, pressing down and coiled to issue power.

双肩锁定, 腰胛扎力。

Both shoulders lock for stability, the waist and scapula coordinate to express power.

落地生根, 龙盘虎踞。

Rooted in the ground, like dragons coil and tigers crouch.

Translator Commentary:

双肩锁定, 腰胛扎力。

Avoid lifting the shoulders, since sunken shoulders provide stability. Coordinate from the bottom up, including movement of the shoulder blades, to add power to your blows.

落地生根, 龙盘虎踞。

Solidify your stance like a tree rooted in the ground, prepared for battle like a Chinese dragon or a tiger coiled and ready to attack.

形不破体, 体不柴势。

Keep the body structure, but the body should not be inflexible.

拳打千遍, 身法自然。

Punch and strike a thousand times, so your body movement can become natural.

Translator Commentary:

形不破体, 体不柴势。

While structure is important, so is mobility. Don't misunderstand the purpose of structure, because it serves both the purposes of stability and mobility.

拳打千遍, 身法自然。

A boxer must practice coordinating the core, footwork and arm movements thousands of times in order for the movements to become smooth, coordinated, and powerful. Isolated training of footwork or arms is primarily for beginners.

> 应接之际，身无定势。
>
> **When it comes to receiving, there are no fixed positions.**
>
> 起身要横，落身要顺。
>
> **When you rise you must be brave, and when you sink you must be smooth.**

Translator Commentary:

应接之际，身无定势。

In real situations, nothing will be identical to your training. You will not encounter the exact same energies, angles, or attacks that you trained against, so you must be able to stretch your training and adapt to changing circumstances.

起身要横，落身要顺。

Lift, and rising are "floating" movements, which carry the risk of being unbalanced. When performing these actions, one must be brave and committed to complete their maneuver without hesitation or interruption.

Sinking actions require smooth movement on the part of the boxer to be effective against opponents.

进步应低，退步须高。
Sink when advancing, float while retreating.

收如伏猫，纵如放虎。
Receive like a reclined cat, unleash like a released tiger.

Translator Commentary:

进步应低，退步须高。

When advancing on an opponent it becomes more important to stabilize one's root to develop a base of support sufficient to issue power.

When a boxer retreats, he should become light and "float" himself in order to move away quickly.

收如伏猫，纵如放虎。

When dealing with an opponent's attacks, receive them with the casual indifference of a cat lying down, but when you counter, unleash your power like a tiger released from a cage.

消闪得机，过解及时。

Evade when there is opportunity, apply solutions timely.

腰则为轴，其转如蓬。

The waist is the axis, and it rotates like a sail.

Translator Commentary:

消闪得机，过解及时。

If you are in a situation where you are being entangled or otherwise controlled, dodge or evade to a new position and apply an alternative solution quickly.

腰则为轴，其转如蓬。

The waist is considered the central hub of human movement. It should rotate flexibly to deal with enemies coming from any direction, the way a sail turns freely to catch the wind.

> 脚手连腰, 如备五弓。
>
> **The feet and hands are connected to the waist, readying the five bows.**
>
> 引而待发, 动不失中。
>
> **Waiting to be launched, do not miss the center.**

Translator Commentary:

脚手连腰, 如备五弓。

The unified and coordinated structure of the arms and the legs are connected through the waist, which powers them. Each of these structures can bend and straighten like a bow, and can be called upon to add power to a boxer's movements.

引而待发, 动不失中。

Keep the body coiled in preparation for action, and when you strike, seek the center.

> 丹田鼓荡, 任督贲张。
>
> **Breath from the dantien, allow the ren and du meridians to be relaxed and vigorous.**
>
> 提肠吊肚, 腰脊聚力。
>
> **Lift the anus, tighten the stomach, and strengthen the lumbar spine.**

Translator Commentary:

丹田鼓荡, 任督贲张。

Breath from the lower abdomen, filling the bottom of the lungs by expanding the lower stomach during inhale, avoiding expansion of the chest.

In acupuncture theory, the Ren and Du two meridians are considered to be the most important and influential, as they run along the center of the body and are thought to regulate the flow of qi and blood throughout the body. Relaxing of the Ren and Du meridians can help to balance the flow of qi and blood, and promote physical, mental, and emotional well-being.

提肠吊肚, 腰脊聚力。

There should be tension in the area of the pelvic girdle, including the contraction of the anus, and tightness of the muscles in the front and back of the lower torso. This tension is helpful in preparation for quick movement, delivering power from the ground to the arms, and in defense against blows, similar to "iron shirt" training.

大椎宜卸, 尾闾中落。
The spine should be straight, with the coccyx centered.

精神气力, 凝集贯通。
Mentally strong, energy penetrates throughout.

Translator Commentary:

大椎宜卸, 尾闾中落。

The vertebrae should be aligned, with the back straight. They should have the feeling of being unloaded and relaxed, with alignment vertical and the tailbone directly below the center of gravity.

精神气力, 凝集贯通。

With the feeling created by maintaining a stable centered posture, a Taizu boxer should feel energized, both mentally and physically.

胯如机枢，闪展赖之。
Body pivots around the crotch, and evasion depends on it.

两胯务夹，谷道宜提。
Both sides of the crotch are clamped for stability, and the anal sphincter is lifted.

Translator Commentary:

胯如机枢，闪展赖之。

Just below the center of gravity, the crotch area is where most whole body movement begins. All fast footwork and body movement including dodging, sinking, rising, pivoting, advancing, and retreating is dependent on this portion of the anatomy.

两胯务夹，谷道宜提。

To move both freely and with power, the adductor muscles must be activated, simultaneous with the contraction of the muscles of the anus and perineum area.

> 步武夹束, 腰骱煞定。
> **Footwork must be constrained, requiring that the waist and crotch are stabilized.**
>
> 连消带闪, 腰骱齐移。
> **When dodging, the waist and crotch move together.**

Translator Commentary:

步武夹束, 腰骱煞定。

For footwork to be effective, the body must be developed in terms of strength, flexibility, coordination, and posture. The biomechanics derived from proper posture, tension, and coordination ultimately guide powerful movement of the Taizu boxer. While the crotch is a central component of strong, stable, and powerful movement, the waist must be firmly stabilized, as the waist is considered the junction between the lower and upper body.

连消带闪, 腰骱齐移。

Because dodging and evading require the coordinated efforts of the upper and lower body, the movements of the waist and crotch must be harmonized to achieve a successful outcome.

就势转化，其势自灵。

Upon receiving momentum rotate and neutralize, the potential is self-evident.

靠打无败，千钧难移。

Undefeated in fighting, and hard to move.

Translator Commentary:

就势转化，其势自灵。

With strong and flexible movements enabled by refined coordination of the movement of the crotch and waist, it becomes possible to deflect incoming energy through rotation of the lower-body, neutralizing attacks, and then countering effectively.

靠打无败，千钧难移。

This ability to move flexibly, with good structure and power, makes it possible to be immovable at will, and victorious against enemies.

Posture of the Arms and Hands

拳不空发，利箭穿革。

The fist is not empty issuing, and the arrow pierces the leather.

手不空回，倒拉九牛。

Hand doesn't return empty, with the strength to pull nine ox.

Translator Commentary:

拳不空发，利箭穿革。

Issuing a punch should be extremely powerful, like an arrow piercing a leather hide.

手不空回，倒拉九牛。

Taizu recommends retracting motions be both useful and powerful. When retracting, if one can pull the opponent off-balance, then the chance of landing a penetrating blow is increased.

A Taizu boxer's pulling power should be like that developed when handling cattle.

> 如戈似盾，蓄发相生。
>
> **Like a dagger and a shield, storing and releasing in cooperation.**
>
> 一技数变，明暗互寓。
>
> **A single skill can change, and techniques can be obvious or ambiguous.**

Translator Commentary:

如戈似盾，蓄发相生。

A Taizu boxer should both alternate and coordinate the left and right, lead and rear hands, such that when one retracts, coiling for the next strike, the other extends to ensure there are no gaps, openings, or missed opportunities.

一技数变，明暗互寓。

Every skill or technique can, and should, be used in a multitude of ways. Some of these methods are obvious, while others are not. A boxer should experiment in their training, stretching techniques for various purposes, exploring all defensive and offensive capabilities of their techniques, all ranges and elevations, and all four of the primary fighting methods (ti, da, shuai, and na).

长贵力足, 直中见曲。

Long, noble, and powerful, straight, but still bend in reserve.

短护八卦, 随曲就直。

Short skills protect the bagua, from bent to straight.

Translator Commentary:

长贵力足, 直中见曲。

Even when striking fully, and extending strike to maximum range, some extension should be reserved. If overly extended, one's momentum and balance can become compromised, and if one's elbow is locked in full extension, it becomes a liability as the opponent might have the skill to damage it. When striking, retain some range of motion to recover or continue to fight and counter.

If necessary, move the lower body in closer, take a larger step forward to ensure the arms don't have to stretch too far.

短护八卦, 随曲就直。

In Fujian martial arts, the chest is sometimes referred to as the "bagua" (eight trigrams), and the bent arms (hands up, elbows down and in front of the chest) protect it. In Southern Chinese martial arts, it is often said the that hands protect the head, the forearms protect the chest, and the elbows protect the body.

When applying close-range boxing movements, the arms alternate from bent to straight quickly to strike out, returning to "bent" once again.

长短互卫, 因势发技。

Long and short defend each other, apply skills according to the situation.

肘不贴肋, 出七留三。

Elbow does not touch the ribs, expend seven and retain three.

Translator Commentary:

长短互卫, 因势发技。

With the influence from the Northern long fist style, and the preferences of Southern short-arm boxing, Taizuquan is comfortable with both long and short range skills

Since long skills can reach the attacker, and defenses only needing reach the practitioner, short and long both have their place, and should be applied in the correct context.

肘不贴肋, 出七留三。

When in the retracted "bent-arm" guard, the Taizu boxer is warned to not let his elbows drop and touch either the front or side of the rib-cage. Having some space between the elbow and torso creates a buffer or "shock-absorber" effect for situations where the arm is receiving a blow from the opponent. If the arm is directly contacting the torso, then the blow will directly impact the torso through the arm.

A practitioner is also advised to not put 100% of their power in any given blow, lest they be taken advantage of, unbalanced, or simply tired out too quickly.

借技而入，技手宜活。

Use "borrowing" skills to enter, skilled hands should be lively.

阴阳要转，吞吐宜明。

Yin and yang should interchange, swallowing and spitting should be obvious.

Translator Commentary:

借技而入，技手宜活。

"Borrowing skills " refers to using the movements and bridges of the opponent to create opportunities to strike, lock, or unbalance him. This kind of skill requires great timing, sensitivity, and adaptability to apply effectively.

阴阳要转，吞吐宜明。

When applying in this way, there will be a fluid interchange of the roles of both hands: in/out, up/down, coiling clockwise vs counter-clockwise, etc., however the pulling (swallowing) and striking (spitting) movements will be more visible to an observer.

意到指到，指到力到。

The mind arrives and the fingers arrive, the fingers arrive and the force arrives.

激力点端，点到即收。

Direct power to vulnerable points, attacking and immediately resetting.

Translator Commentary:

意到指到，指到力到。

Taizu boxers place emphasis on the mind's intention (yi) and how it drives the actions of the limbs. Where the mind wills the body, the body follows. If the boxer wills the fingers to find a vital spot, first the target acquisition occurs, then the issuance of power into the point happens.

激力点端，点到即收。

When attacking vital points, its important to attack and then quickly relax in order to immediately defend, strike again, or otherwise continue to control and overwhelm the attacker.

手杯如刀，俯仰为用。

The hand can be like a knife, applied in a shape according to the situation.

利刀削竹，随技而变。

Like a sharp knife peeling bamboo, follow the situation and change to the needed skill.

Translator Commentary:

手杯如刀，俯仰为用。

Like a knife blade which has a spine, a tip, and a variable curve along its cutting edge, the human hand has different surfaces, each with different utility.

利刀削竹，随技而变。

The boxer is advised to change the shape and use of the hand according to the context, like the various parts of the knife are used when peeling the skin from a bamboo pole.

腕坐而挡, 节暴而懔。

The wrist sits and blocks, the segments are violent and quick.

一粘即发, 一沉即脱。

Once sticky immediately issue, when sunk immediately escape.

Translator Commentary:

腕坐而挡, 节暴而懔。

Given the style of guard used by a Taizu boxer, it becomes possible to drop the wrist on incoming attacks and quickly counter from that position. Striking downward with the wrist, as well as striking with the elbow is done with violent action, with the goal of damaging the opponent even when merely defending their blows.

一粘即发, 一沉即脱。

The Taizu boxer is given recommendations for dealing with specific situations that might occur:

- If the opponent becomes "sticky", following and pressing without a gap, then immediately strike out, issuing force to break their "sticky" control.
- Should the opponent trap and sink you, then immediately release yourself and escape.

拳须归中，拳对心槽。

The fist returns to the center, the fist defends the tanzhong point.

心槽对鼻，内气方聚。

The tanzhong aligned to the nose, and the inner qi is gathered.

Translator Commentary:

拳须归中，拳对心槽。

Taizu boxers prefer to keep the hands in front of the middle of the body, to protect the vitals, and to have the ability to extend either high or low and have a middle location to return to quickly.

心槽对鼻，内气方聚。

It is believed that keeping the nose generally aligned with the center of the body helps with the accumulation of qi.

The tanzhong point:

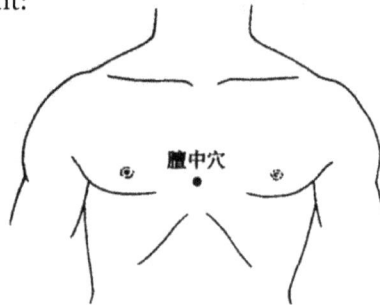

膻中穴

前节肢柔, 拳尾力刚。

The front section is flexible, the end of the punch is strong.

近身而发, 防不胜防。

Closing the distance to issue, it's hard to guard against.

Translator Commentary:

前节肢柔, 拳尾力刚。

The "front section" is comprised of the wrist, hand, and fingers. Fujian boxers like to indicate the liveliness of this aspect of arm movement, likening it to a dragon playing in the water, or a tiger catching a pig.

This liveliness is considered flexible or "soft". Even though the hand is flexible, the punch is strong and hard. This comment is pointing out the dual nature of the hand from a soft/hard perspective.

近身而发, 防不胜防。

Since the preference of a Taizu boxer is to close the gap, the liveliness of the hands makes it very difficult for the opponent to put up an adequate defense.

Posture of the Lower Body

不丁不八，尺八为度。

Not "ding", not "bu", one foot eight inches is the measurement.

前三后七，下盘轻固。

Stance is three-seven, the lower body is both light and firm.

Translator Commentary:

不丁不八，尺八为度。

"Not ding, not bu" is a common phrase in Southern Chinese martial arts, describing a stance where the feet are not fully describing a "T" shape, and not fully a "pidgeon-toed" stance.

Depending on the style and teacher, this may indicate:

- **the rear foot pointing forward and the lead foot turned in,**
- the front foot pointing forward and the rear foot turned out, or
- the front foot turned in and the rear foot turned out

The recommended distance between the feet is one foot, eight inches.

前三后七，下盘轻固。

The stance is typically rear-weighted, such that the rear leg supports 70% of the body weight with the lead leg only supporting the remaining 30%. This method supports the quick use of the lead leg for kicking, and the lightness of the lead leg assists in escaping sweeping maneuvers aimed at it.

The practitioner is advised to keep the lower body both relaxed and stable, relaxed to move quickly as necessary, but stable enough to support the upper body adequately.

脚弓兜入, 前臁着力。

Front foot is turned inward, the lower leg is strengthened.

脚尖对膝, 膝对肚脐。

Toes to knees, knees to navel.

Translator Commentary:

脚弓兜入, 前臁着力。

Because of the close-in and front-facing nature of Taizuquan, there is a risk of being kicked in the groin, perineum, bladder, etc. The stance used to combat this has the lead leg (foot and kneed) turned in to help close off these vital points.

脚尖对膝, 膝对肚脐。

When using the leg in defense of these targets, the typical response is to lift the lead leg up and toward the centerline, finishing in a position where the toes of the lead leg are level with the knee of the rear leg which puts the knee of the lead leg level with the belly-button.

后脚坐实, 规身添扎。

Sit firmly on the back foot, supporting the regulation of the whole body.

步武不长, 脚马硬箭。

Stepping is not large, footwork is strong and direct.

Translator Commentary:

后脚坐实, 规身添扎。

With 70% of the boxer's weight typically on the rear leg, he must find comfort in finding and maintaining the balance for the body. This weight distribution must become natural in the movement of both the upper and lower bodies.

步武不长, 脚马硬箭。

Stepping in Taizu is often performed in short, shuffling movements, rather than larger pass-thru steps that risk having the feet gathered closely, vulnerable to a double-leg sweep.

These shorter pressing, shuffling steps allow the Taizu boxer to maintain a strong base, while pressing ever forward.

三金落地, 五趾抓实。

Three points of gold drop to the earth, and the five toes grip firmly.

脚肚吊硬, 中脊凝气。

Calf contracts forcefully, and the mid-spine solidifies the (yang) qi.

Translator Commentary:

三金落地, 五趾抓实。

As the foot is shaped roughly like a triangle, all edges of the foot should remain in contact with the ground, while the toes should grab the floor to add increased surface area and stability to the foot.

脚肚吊硬, 中脊凝气。

Maintain power in the lower leg as well as the mid-back.

> 执步如钉, 立如金刚。
>
> **Stable as if nailed down, standing like a Vajra warrior.**
>
> 夹束如铁, 力贯于地。
>
> **Clamped like iron, force emanates the ground.**

Translator Commentary:

执步如钉, 立如金刚。

The stability of the Taizu boxer is an essential aspect of their martial arts practice, and it is something that is emphasized and refined through training. By maintaining a solid base, the Taizu boxer is better equipped to deliver powerful strikes, as well as to withstand the force of an opponent's attacks. This stability allows them to remain upright and in control, even in the heat of battle.

The Vajra warriors, on the other hand, are depicted as imposing figures, standing guard at Buddhist temples. Their appearance is meant to inspire fear and reverence in those who pass by, and their statues serve as a reminder of the power and strength that lies within.

夹束如铁, 力贯于地。

Taizu boxers should utilize the adductor muscles the create an inward, squeezing force between the feet. This inward tension helps provide strength and stability to stance.

With the rear leg firmly grounded, the practitioner should push downward, creating the ability to transfer the "ground-reaction force" into the power of their strikes.

> 步武重后，如虎蹲踞。
>
> **When stepping the back foot is heavy, like a tiger crouched.**
>
> 前脚轻迈，如猫弧出。
>
> **The front leg steps lightly, like a cat reaching out.**

Translator Commentary:

This series of statements is meant to highlight the differences between the rear and front legs using the comparison of two different kinds of cats.

步武重后，如虎蹲踞。

A tiger is large and heavy, and uses its weight to drag down prey. This heaviness is felt in the back leg, and the muscles of the leg are coiled and poised for explosive movement and transfer of power to the upper body.

前脚轻迈，如猫弧出。

Conversely, smaller cats reach forward gingerly with their front legs to find a spot on the ground that will enable it to stealthily track prey. This lightness in the front leg allows it to be agile and adaptive to the circumstances.

> 以骱运脚, 进退自如。
> **As the crotch directs the legs, move forward and back freely.**
>
> 技手如动, 步必随之。
> **If the hand moves, the step will follow.**

Translator Commentary:

以骱运脚, 进退自如。

In contrast with Northern Chinese martial arts that focus on the hips and lumbar region (kua 胯), Fujian martial arts discuss the crotch (骱), the muscles of the inner hip and thigh area, as the primary engine that drives the movement of the core and legs.

Mastery of these muscles is believed to be the key to unlocking powerful and fluid movement.

技手如动, 步必随之。

Practitioners are advised to coordinate the upper and lower body, so they can support, power, defend, and enhance one another.

脚马不稳, 上卦必虚。

If the stances are unstable, the upper body will be empty.

转换不灵, 攻守失机。

Turning and exchanging is sluggish, offense and defense are lost opportunities.

Translator Commentary:

脚马不稳, 上卦必虚。

Further describing the need to have strong, stable and coordinated upper and lower bodies, the boxer is warned that the upper body will be hampered if the lower body isn't solid.

转换不灵, 攻守失机。

Not only might the boxer fail in defense and not be able to counter-strike effectively, but a weak horse (stance) will limit his ability to apply needed evasive and crowding footwork.

脚力煞定, 灵动其身。

When the leg strength is stable, then the body can be lively.

慢则易制, 浮则无根。

Slow is easy to control, and floating has no root.

Translator Commentary:

脚力煞定, 灵动其身。

Leg strength provides increases *stability*, while supporting *agility*. Both opposing capabilities are fueled by strong legs.

慢则易制, 浮则无根。

Speed and agility are important attributes leading to effective counter-control. Without them, the opponent will likely succeed.

The same is true if one is not rooted. Losing control of, or mismanaging, one's center of gravity is a recipe for failure.

> 灵中见稳, 动中求固。
> **Find stability in liveliness, and movement in the solid.**
>
> 踢不过脐, 近身加膝。
> **Don't kick above the navel, when close use knees.**

Translator Commentary:

灵中见稳, 动中求固。

Seek to root quickly after moving, in order to be able to receive or issue power immediately.

Also, when rooted, explore the limits of safe movement while maintaining your base of support. Test your strength within your functional range of movement in each stance and learn to apply each stance, position, and angle for its best effect.

踢不过脐, 近身加膝。

Kicking high creates numerous risks, including "floating" one's self and opening the groin for attack, so kicking below the opponent's navel is recommended. Ideal targets are the bladder, the groin, inside of the thigh, all surfaces of the knee, the ankle, and the top of the foot. When too close to attack the targets between the opponent's navel and knee, use your own knee to attack.

武林館

4

Qi, Breath, Power, and Coordination

气水养力, 纳气深长。

Stamina and endurance nourish strength, inhale deep and long.

气水持长, 力草饱满。

For stamina and endurance to be long-lasting, strength must be cultivated.

Translator Commentary:

气水养力, 纳气深长。

Strength and endurance are related, since sufficient strength accomplishes tasks with less overall effort. Breath is critical to energy production, so breath control is of paramount importance in driving the body's ability to issue power.

气水持长, 力草饱满。

Conversely, building strength helps to increase stamina as a byproduct. Building strength helps stabilize posture, contributes to agility, helps to build endurance, and is the primary attribute necessary to developing refined power.

气沉丹田，蓄气盈盈。

Breath sinks into the lower dantian, accumulating to abundance.

善蓄力足，善运力恒。

Good at accumulating strength, consistently good at transporting power.

Translator Commentary:

气沉丹田，蓄气盈盈。

When breathing, one must endeavor to breath fully, into the lower part of the lungs, filling the lungs to capacity without expanding the chest.

善蓄力足，善运力恒。

When one can breath properly, energy will flow, and power the strength needed in every part of the body.

中气宜透，闷气劳伤。

Breathing must be smooth, or suffer from suffocation and fatigue.

守则气虚，动则气喘。

With a qi deficiency, moving will cause loss of breath.

Translator Commentary:

中气宜透，闷气劳伤。

Boxers must take care to regulate their breath. Holding the breath, failing to breath, breathing from the chest, or panting haphazardly can all lead to a lack of stamina due to a lack of oxygen or buildup of carbon dioxide.

守则气虚，动则气喘。

In cases where the air isn't regulated properly, any activity can cause the boxer to become winded and starved of strength.

纳息吐气, 徐疾自然。

Take in the breath, and exhale the qi, slowly and naturally.

鼻纳口吐, 长吸短呼。

The nose inhales and the mouth exhales, use a long inhale and short exhale.

Translator Commentary:

纳息吐气, 徐疾自然。

Boxers should practice the slow and natural method of inhaling and exhaling.

鼻纳口吐, 长吸短呼。

Inhale through the nose and exhale through the mouth. The inhale will be slower, due to the smaller nasal openings, while the exhale can be shorter.

規身环行, 力气两全。

Regulate and circle the body, have both strength and qi everywhere.

腰动生力, 发借地力。

The waist is vigorous, issuing borrows the power of the earth.

Translator Commentary:

规身环行, 力气两全。

When the breath is abundant, qi can circle the body and be transported where needed, and strength will be enhanced.

腰动生力, 发借地力。

With the body fully energized, it can utilize the waist to redirect the ground-reaction force into the opponent.

咬起牙关, 牙欲断筋。
Grit the teeth, they want to break tendons.

舌欲顶齿, 发欲冲冠。
Tongue presses the upper teeth, and anger rushes to the crown.

Translator Commentary:

咬起牙关, 牙欲断筋。

When facing an opponent, clench the teeth as if one were attempting to bite through connective tissue.

舌欲顶齿, 发欲冲冠。

Keep the tongue pressed against the upper palate, as this assists the energy circulation of the head, and management of the excitement of the adrenal response.

指欲透骨，掌欲推山。

The fingers want to penetrate bone, the palm wants to push the mountain.

运腰发力，力发到额。

Move the waist to express force, the amount is regulated.

Translator Commentary:

指欲透骨，掌欲推山。

A Taizu boxer must develop the power and toughness of the body, so the fingers can penetrate deeply in the cavities between bones to strike at vital points, and the palms can push powerfully to knock down opponents.

运腰发力，力发到额。

The body's power is focused, coordinated, and regulated by the waist which connects the structure and power of the lower body with the structure and acceleration of the upper body. This helps create the force needed, without letting the body move haphazardly, missing the mark or over-extending.

手与脚合，肘与膝合。

Hands and feet coordinate, as do the elbows and knees.

肩与胯合，三合四配。

Shoulders and the crotch are also coordinated, making the three external harmonies and four sets.

Translator Commentary:

手与脚合，肘与膝合。

The pairings of the hands and feet, elbows and knees, and the shoulders and crotch are called the "external three harmonies". When the corresponding sections of the upper and lower body are working together, the structure is stabilized and movement is powerful.

肩与胯合，三合四配。

When the external three harmonies are developed, the four limbs work in smooth and powerful coordination.

> 梢节初起，中关相随。
> **The first section is the beginning, the middle section follows.**
>
> 根节紧追，劲道顺遂。
> **The root section chases closely, and the power flows smoothly.**

Translator Commentary:

梢节初起，中关相随。

Even though power is expressed from the ground up, through the body, one sees the hand move first, powered by the elbow.

根节紧追，劲道顺遂。

The shoulder pushes the elbow, and smoothly expresses the energy into the hand, which is the point of contact, while the body is the source of power.

神与气合，劲力乃生。

When the shen and qi are combined, strength is born.

抄肠刮肚，丹田运气。

Lifting intestines and moving the belly, the dantian transports the qi.

Translator Commentary:

神与气合，劲力乃生。

In traditional Chinese medicine, the "three treasures" of essence (jing), breath / energy (qi), and spirit (shen) must be cultivated and managed. Important to the development of refined strength are the combination of breath energy and the spirit to produce explosive power.

抄肠刮肚，丹田运气。

In order to move the breath energy from the dan tien to where it will be utilized in the body, one must contract and expand as well as open and close the lower abdomen, which house the intestines.

运气发力, 气行催力。
Transport qi to issue force, move the qi to expedite strength.

内劲聚发, 浑然贯穿。
Inner strength is gathered, when issued...penetrates fully.

Translator Commentary:

运气发力, 气行催力。

One must move the qi to where it is needed in order to strengthen the body, and utilize the breath to encourage the issuing of power.

内劲聚发, 浑然贯穿。

Gathering and storing the energy is accomplished through inhalation, and when used, can assist in fully penetrating the enemy's defense.

劲力贵脆, 刚柔相寓。

Strength is precious and crisp, due to hardness and softness coexisting.

节力换劲, 利贯始终。

Exchanging force, the benefits are consistent.

Translator Commentary:

劲力贵脆, 刚柔相寓。

A Taizu boxer prizes "crisp" power which issues quickly and retracts cleanly. The balance of hardness and softness is central to a boxer's ability to defend and counter an opponent.

节力换劲, 利贯始终。

Exerting and relaxing must be managed in turn, to avoid exhaustion, to increase explosive power, and to adapt to changing situations. The benefits of alternating from tense to relaxed are many, and boxers should study this deeply.

5

Essential Strategies and Tactics

料敌机先, 临敌势变。

First predict the enemy's plan, but adapt to the changing situation.

审势立策, 待时寻机。

Judge the situation and form a strategy, look for opportunities while waiting.

Translator Commentary:

料敌机先, 临敌势变。

While planning is not always possible, but when available, the opportunity shouldn't be squandered. Adaptability is important in all contexts.

审势立策, 待时寻机。

If presented with an opportunity to observe before acting, take advantage of the occasion to become better prepared for action.

Taizu recommends both approaches…pre-planning when possible and just-in-time adaptability when necessary.

> 以静待动, 固守待进。
>
> **Use stillness to wait for action, stand guarded and wait for progress.**
>
> 静无常形, 动如雷霆。
>
> **Avoid giving clues to your shape, and then move like thunderclap.**

Translator Commentary:

以静待动, 固守待进。

Taizuquan recommends against moving hastily and without purpose, instead recommending the practitioner gauge the situation and act when the moment for action is clear.

静无常形, 动如雷霆。

Don't provide an opponent an opportunity to assess you in the same way...remain conservative until acting and then move explosively.

閃空疾入, 伺机进击。

Evade and quickly enter a gap, after waiting for the opportunity to attack.

旧力已过, 新力未生。

The old force has passed, and the new force has not yet arisen.

Translator Commentary:

闪空疾入, 伺机进击。

If attacked while assessing the opponent, evade their blow and enter where safe…this could be via the side door (flank), or above or below the attacker's bridge.

旧力已过, 新力未生。

This statement likely derives from the writings of famous general Yu Dayao.

Yu indicates that the prime opportunity to counter is just as the opponent's attacking energy has been expended, and before they can defend or continue to attack.

> 寻其拍位, 后发制人。
> **Find the timing, then counter-attack.**
>
> 柔承力尾, 刚在力前。
> **Softly if late, forcibly if early.**

Translator Commentary:

寻其拍位, 后发制人。

Timing is critical in a counter-attacking methodology, so learning how to find the gap in the opponent's timing is a valuable skill.

柔承力尾, 刚在力前。

If there is an opportunity to lead the initiative, attack strongly, but if one has lost the initiative, redirect and flow with the attack and find a way to counter indirectly.

刚近枯槁，柔有生意
Hard is nearly withered, soft still has vitality.

齿以刚折，舌以柔存。
Teeth are hard and break, the tongue is soft and survives.

Translator Commentary:

刚近枯槁，柔有生意

As softness is often difficult for the young and strong to appreciate, these poems attempt to explain the value and strength of softness. This section is a reference to plants…dried and hard vs soft and full of life.

齿以刚折，舌以柔存。

This is a popular saying among Fujian martial traditions regarding the effects of old age. As you age, your teeth (though hard) are lost, while the soft tongue is unaffected by the years.

强则化之, 以柔克刚
Strong but neutralized, as soft can control hard.

弱则逼之, 以刚克柔。
Weak but forced, as hard can control soft.

Translator Commentary:

强则化之, 以柔克刚

The first section describes that "soft" fighting methods (redirection and other non-striking maneuvers) can be used to neutralize control hard fighting methods (typically strikes and kicks).

弱则逼之, 以刚克柔。

The second section reminds the practitioner that softness can also be overpowered.

The combination of these statements is meant to be a reminder that both soft and hard methods are important to understand and implement, as each can be countered.

Proficiency in only one aspect can easily lead to the practitioner's defeat.

运柔顾己, 使刚克敌。
Use soft to mind yourself, use hard to control the enemy.

以柔济刚, 阴阳互化。
Use softness to aid hard, yin and yang mutually transform.

Translator Commentary:

运柔顾己, 使刚克敌。

This is a reminder that many defensive maneuvers can be considered soft, taking into account redirection, absorption, and flow involved, while most attacking methods are easily labeled "hard".

以柔济刚, 阴阳互化。

Soft, yielding methods can create good opportunities for decisive and powerful finishing maneuvers,

Because soft and hard methods can counter, as well as support one another, the ability to change and adapt to utilize the methods appropriate to the current context is the highest level of skill.

中官抢进, 边门闪赚

Charge through the middle, or deceive by evading into the side door.

身手相随, 势挟风雨。

Body and hand go together, with momentum like the arrival of wind and rain.

Translator Commentary:

中官抢进, 边门闪赚

While Taizu practitioners have a preference for charging through the center gate, they are equally aware that evading and entering from the flank is an important option.

It's common that inexperienced, low-skill or timid practitioners prefer to enter via the flank, while those who have developed experience, skill, and courage are more comfortable fighting "head-on".

身手相随, 势挟风雨。

When fighting, Taizu boxers should unify the movement of the body and hands, overwhelming opponents.

This effect is likened to a fierce rainstorm, with winds whipping from different directions and varying sheets of rain obstruction vision.

紧如狂风，叠如骤雨
Pressing like violent wind, overwhelming like a cloudburst.

以速御迟，紧叠难防。
Use speed to defeat the sluggish, overwhelming combinations are hard to defend against.

Translator Commentary:
紧如狂风，叠如骤雨

Continuing the analogy of overwhelming action, the Taizu practitioner's movements are expected to be violent and overwhelming like the wind and rain.

以速御迟，紧叠难防。

While timing is important, pure speed is considered to be one of the more important physical attributes necessary to overwhelm an opponent.

The ability for a Taizu boxer to apply fast combinations make it exceedingly difficult for an opponent to counter.

木实易摧, 竹空难折
Solid wood is easy to break, bamboo is not.

以虚诱实, 乘虚而入。
Use the false to entice the real, take advantage of the false to enter.

Translator Commentary:

木实易摧, 竹空难折

Bamboo is touted for its ability to flex rather than break, and for a Taizu boxer, this is a reminder to stay mobile and flexible. If one remains a fixed, rooted target an attacker is more likely to land a penetrating blow.

以虚诱实, 乘虚而入。

Using the "false" or "virtual" to entice, manage, or control the "real" is a core strategy which constitutes baiting or otherwise tricking an opponent to either attack a target that is, in truth, well-protected, or fall victim to a feint which opens up an opportunity to enter and control an opponent.

There are many tactics involving indirect attacks or other clever maneuvers which fall under the strategy of "using the false to control the real".

> 声东击西, 避实就虚。
>
> **Make a noise in the East and attack the West, avoid strength and attack weakness.**
>
> 乘他力尾, 打他力头。
>
> **Take advantage of expended strength, hit before he recovers.**

Translator Commentary:

声东击西, 避实就虚。

One of the oldest written strategies is to "make a sound in the East, and strike the West", which is a clear indication of a feint maneuver.

To avoid the solid and attack the void is to flow around obstructions or enter gaps in the opponent's defenses and find a target.

乘他力尾, 打他力头。

As previously discussed, one of the most vulnerable moments for an attacker is when their power is expended, so quickly hit before he can regain his strength and posture.

有桥过桥，无桥造桥。
If you have a bridge...cross it, if not then build it.

有桥断桥，无桥离桥。
If you control the bridge...break it, if you don't...leave it.

Translator Commentary:

有桥过桥，无桥造桥。

In Southern Chinese martial arts, a "bridge" is a situation where the practitioner and opponent's arms are touching, as when one blocks a punch.

The advice here is:

- When a useful bridge has been created, quickly "cross" the bridge to attack the opponent's head or torso.
- If a bridge doesn't yet exist, directly attacking the head or body may be too dangerous, resulting in the practitioner being hit, therefore creating a bridge before entering too close is advised.

有桥断桥，无桥离桥。

Continuing with the advice for "bridged" arm scenarios:

- If there is a bridge, you may want to damage the arm, break the elbow, etc.
- If the bridge is not advantageous, then separate from it, removing contact with the opponent, lest he use it to his advantage.

6

Closing Remarks

韬略在心, 功夫在手
Strategy is in the mind, gong fu is in the hand.

心领实练, 明而神之。
The minds leads the training, understandable and extraordinary.

Translator Commentary:
韬略在心, 功夫在手

The author takes this opportunity, after explaining a tremendous amount of boxing-related theory, to remind the reader that gong fu…actual skill…must be developed through training, so it doesn't live in the realm of mental theory, but it becomes actualized in practitioner's hand.

Poems, history, and theory are critical in understanding the past and guiding training and teaching methods, but they will never replace actual training.

心领实练, 明而神之。

Again, the theory takes root in the mind, which then leads the training and teaching methods, which should be clearly understandable, yet profound.

> 余非能文, 亦非善武
> **I am neither capable of writing, nor good at martial arts.**
>
> 太祖拳略, 系余杜撰。
> **This "Taizu boxing brief", created by Zeng Jinbu.**

Translator Commentary:
余非能文, 亦非善武

The author takes this opportunity to demonstrate humility in both his writing and martial skills.

太祖拳略, 系余杜撰。

The author names the writing, and credits himself with the writing.

> 搜索枯肠，案牍劳形。
>
> **At the risk of embarrassment, with labor this document took shape.**
>
> 编集是言，留赠郑君。
>
> **This compilation is a statement, a distillation for Zheng Lianlai.**

Translator Commentary:

搜索枯肠，案牍劳形。

The author knew there were risks with going through the effort of researching and documenting the contents of this treatise. Some authors of such treatise are berated by peers and/or seniors for making such "secrets" public.

编集是言，留赠郑君。

Here, the author indicates that he documented this valuable information for his student, Zheng Lianlai.

武之一道，亦宜精讲。
In martial arts, explanations should be refined.

试录于兹，以赠后学。
Try to follow what is recorded here, it is a gift for later learning.

君等鉴之，勿作妄谈。
Please examine it, don't make false comments.

Translator Commentary:

武之一道，亦宜精讲。

The author makes the case here, that boxing maxims should be clear and well-understood.

试录于兹，以赠后学。

He entreats the reader, to follow it's advice and return to it during the process of learning, knowing that readers will glean more and more from future readings as their boxing experience increases.

君等鉴之，勿作妄谈。

Here, the author implores future generations of practitioners to use this guide to keep the core concepts of the system intact, in order to avoid changes and misunderstandings due to misstatements.

About the Translator

Practicing karate since the 1980's, Russ Smith had a keen interest in the influences of Southern Chinese martial arts on the origins of karate.

Seeking out teachers and training opportunities to better understand karate, over the last four decades Russ has made numerous trips overseas to train in karate and kobudo in Okinawa, and several styles of Fujian gung fu in Malaysia, Singapore, and the Philippines.

Russ was fortunate to have met Sifu Mark Wiley, who exposed him to the depth and breadth of Five Ancestor boxing as taught to him by his good friend, and teacher, Sifu Alex Co. Russ is the Chairman and Archivist of the International Beng Hong Association.

Russ's current focus is preserving, promoting, and researching the martial traditions of Southern China, Okinawa, and the Philippines at **Burinkan Martial Arts**.

Russ is honored to have many wonderful friends, mentors, teachers, and students throughout the world-wide martial arts community.

6th generation Instructor - Five Ancestor boxing

6th generation Instructor - Goju-ryu Karate

4th generation Instructor - Matayoshi Kobudo

8th generation Instructor - White Eyebrow

Sources / References

Chen, Huoyu. *Nan Shao Lin Wu Zu Quan*. Taibei Shi: Da Zhan Chu Ban She You Xian Gong Si, 2012. Print.

Co, Alexander L. *The Way of Ngo Cho Kun Kung Fu*. Jafaha Publications, 1983

Co, Alexander L. *Five Ancestor Fist Kung-fu: The Way of Ngo Cho Kun*. Rutland, VT: Charles E. Tuttle, 1997. Print.

Gang, Li. *He Quan Shu Zhen*. Tai Bei: Yi Wen Wu Zhu Wen Hua You Xian Gong Si, 2011. Print.

Han, Jin Yuan. *Fundamentals of Nan Shaolin Wuzuquan*, Vols 1-8, First Edition. Print.

Ku, Yuchan. *Five Ancestor Boxing Essentials*. Unknown, 2000. Print.

Ku, Yuchan. *Hong Kong Wushu Master: Ku Yuchan*. Unknown, 2000. Print.

Li, Zailuan. *Fu Jian He Quan Mi Yao*. Xin Bei Shi: Wu Zhou, 2011. Print.

Liang, Weiming. *Zhongguo Wu Gong Tu Dian = Iconographic Dictionary of Chinese Traditional Kung-fu*. Xianggang: Tian He Chuan Bo Chu Ban You Xian Gong Si, 2010. Print.

Liu, Yin Shan. *(Chinese) White Crane Gate. Feeding Crane Boxing*. 1973. Print.

Liu, Yin Shan. *(Chinese) Feeding Crane Secrets*. Print.

Liu, Gu, and Yu-zhang Su. *Bai He Men Shi He Quan*. Tai Bei Xian Zhong He Shi: Wu Zhou, 2005. Print.

Nisan, David S. *The General Tian Wubeizhi: the Bubishi in Chinese Martial Arts History*. Lionbooks Martial Arts Co, 2016. Print.

Pan, Changan. *White Crane Sacred Hand*. 2008. Print.

Smith, Russ. *Principle-Driven Skill Development*. Tambuli Media. 2018 Print.

Su, Yinghan. *Yong Chun White Crane Boxing Overview*. Xiamen University Press,
2016. Print.

Wang, Yi Ying. *Minghe Quanpu (Shouting Crane Boxing Manual)*. Print.

Watts, Martin. *Yong Chun White Crane Kung Fu*. Lulu Press. 2017. Print.

Wu, Feng. *South Family Crane Boxing Applications and Drills*. 2015. Print.

Xin, Chaoshe. *Fu Jian Shao Lin Quan*. Tai Bei Shi: Xin Chao She Chu Ban, 1994 Print.

Zheng, Kunming and Zheng, Lianlai. *Quánzhōu shàolín gǔ quán pǔ zhù yì*. Xiamen University Press. 1996. Print.

Zhou, Kunmin. *Wuzumen Yanjiu*. Forbidden City Publishing House. 1998. Print.

Zhou, Mengyuan. *Wuzuquan Wenhua Yanjiu*. Xiamen University Press. 2012.

Zhou, Mengyuan. *Wuzuquan Huizong*. 2020. Print.

www.ingramcontent.com/pod-product-compliance
Lightning Source LLC
Chambersburg PA
CBHW070056100426
42740CB00013B/2852